This book belongs to

_____

Illustrated by Michael Kelly

Inspired by Grant Wallace

In the small town of Stench

there lived a nose name Snoz.

Snoz was a rather large nose

who was happy, but, at times

could get a little down.

Located right in the middle
of town, for over 100 years,
proudly stood the Ole Factory.

The town is perfect for noses
as it is full of wonderful,
and some not so
wonderful smells.

Mom   Me   Nosey
       (Snoz)

Snoz has lived his entire life in Stench
with his mother and his little brother Nosey.
Nosey could be a bit of a nosey nose, but,
Snoz loved his little brother.

Next door lived his best friends the twins Sniffle and Snort.

Snoz, Nosey, and the twins have all been friends since they were baby noses.

On occasion,
Snoz could get
a little grumpy.

He did not think
being a nose was
very important.

"why can't
we be
eyes
or ears,
Snoz
said to
Sniffle
and Snort.

Even feet
would be
better.

One thing that did make Snoz happy was running.

He put on his sneakers and ran everyday.
It was fun to run past
the powerful smells of Stench.

Snoz would run by the bakery and breathe in the aroma of cinnamon rolls one day and apple pie the next.

Running through the town park he loved the scent of blooming roses, pine trees, and sometimes the odor of fresh cut grass.

When Snoz passes his favorite Pizza place he would catch a whiff of baking crust, rich sauce, fresh vegetables, and melting cheese.

He would even run by the
Ole Factory and get a whiff
of the stinky smoke pouring
out of the chimneys.

That was one smell he
did not like very much.

One day, Snoz
stopped smelling.

"Mom, he said, I woke up today and
I can't smell anything."

After a few days Snoz still could not smell. His mother took him to the doctor who did not find anything wrong.

As he ran through Stench, he did not smell the trees or the freshly cut grass.

Amazingly he did not even get a whiff of the smoke as he jogged past the Ole Factory.

There was no sweet scent of rolls coming from the bakery.

After many days of not
being able to smell
anything, Snoz was
beginning to get sad.

"I guess I was wrong about
noses, he said to the twins.
Life is not very interesting
with no smells."

The very next day Snoz woke up and went for his usual run through Stench.

While running he began to get his smell back.
When he ran past the Ole Factory he got a nose
full of the familiar, but, yucky odor.

On this day, Snoz thought it was the most wonderful smell in the world.

He was happy to be a nose.

The
End

Made in the USA
San Bernardino, CA
06 February 2016